THE ROCKY ROAD TO FREEDOM

Brian Redmond
The Rocky Road To Freedom

All rights reserved
Copyright © 2024 by **Brian Redmond**

No part of this publication may be reproduced, distributed, or transmitted in any form or by any means, including photocopying, recording, or other electronic or mechanical methods, without the prior written permission of the publisher, except in the case of brief quotations embodied in critical reviews and certain other noncommercial uses permitted by copyright law.

Published by Spines
ISBN: 979-8-89569-808-2

THE ROCKY ROAD TO FREEDOM

BRIAN REDMOND

CHAPTER 1

It was a cold December day when I entered the military on the 29th of 1986. I was excited to get away from home, eager to be part of something bigger—I thought that something was the United States Army.

I told no one I had enlisted until a week before my departure. My grandfather had passed away in July of 1985, leaving my grandmother and me without the protection he provided. They were the only parents I ever knew, raising me from infancy, albeit as a spoiled child. I received everything I desired, which was both a curse and a blessing.

I remember an Army recruiter taking me and a few other guys to the airport for our departure to basic training. What fascinated me most was looking out of the airport's huge windows, watching airplanes land and ascend into the crescent city sky. I had some fear of flying, but I was more excited because this would be my first time on an airplane.

As I watched, I thought to myself that flying aboard a 747 would be something else—if I survived. When I saw the small plane we were going to fly on, I wondered if we would even make it. I always believed that smaller planes with propellers had a higher chance of something going wrong; I knew that was a negative mindset, lacking faith. I later realized that thinking positively is far less stressful. At just 18 years old, I was naive and judgmental about many things, and I'm still working on that today.

I boarded the plane filled with fear, wondering what the hell I had gotten myself into. The noise on the runway was deafening, but it grew even louder once we were airborne. The plane shook, and we hit turbulence throughout the flight—yes, I was scared. But we arrived, and I survived. If I hadn't, I wouldn't have had the chance to share any of the experiences I've had since. Before that flight, I had faced worse fears, and between then and now, I've encountered many more.

CHAPTER 2

I stepped off the plane at a small airport in Lawton, Oklahoma. There were others there, and I assumed more would be arriving. Everyone present seemed committed, while those who didn't show up clearly didn't want to be there. At that moment, I wished I was one of them.

Our battery consisted of four platoons, each with four sections of five soldiers. You do the math. We were a diverse group, made up of different races, beliefs, and attitudes. To my left and right, I noticed three or four cattle trucks and thought to myself, "Why do they have cattle trucks at this airport? Are they flying livestock out of here?"

We lined up with our luggage, wearing confused expressions. I had about three full bags that I had to carry everywhere I was directed that day. To my surprise, when word spread that those cattle trucks were our transportation to Fort Sill, I realized there wouldn't be any seats. They were designed for livestock, not human beings. This was one of many degradations I would encounter in the military, and more were soon to follow. Those who have experienced physical and mental abuse know what I'm talking about.

After a horrible ten-minute ride, packed together as if we were animals being transported for slaughter, we arrived at the base. My initial notion of the military was that we were a team, united to fight enemies both foreign and domestic, dedicated to protecting freedom while respecting human rights. I knew I would face challenges; we all do, whether in the military or civilian life.

One of my major challenges came from an incident that changed my entire life: the physical and mental abuse I experienced during basic training from another soldier—my teammate, my ally, my right and left hand in battle—someone going through the same training I was. During the orientation process, we filled out numerous forms detailing our life history and education. I remember opting out of the G.I. Bill for education, not realizing how it could have furthered my academic pursuits. My mindset was, "I tried college, and it wasn't for me." I was young and, most definitely, not focused.

CHAPTER 3

At that time, my focus was on girls and having fun. As I got older, I realized how important an education is. Later in life, I became interested in political science. I still want to be a lawyer, and I'm blessed to say that God has given me the opportunity to pursue that career.

The second day of basic training went fairly well. After we settled in, everyone was getting organized—"dress right, dress!" There was a lot of chattering, and I heard soldiers asking each other what states they were from. I joined in the mingling, but then I caught a strange look from one of the soldiers. He was a big guy, twice my size. I was really skinny and had no idea he would become my perpetrator in the upcoming incident.

I remember the chattering stopping abruptly when two drill sergeants walked in. I won't use their real names, but they were checking for anything we weren't supposed to have. I had an illegal item—a camera. When one of the drill sergeants mentioned it, I made a smart remark in reply, which evidently pissed him off. He threw all my belongings out of the second-floor window, including my bed and mattress.

I couldn't believe that my words could trigger such rage. I had to walk downstairs to recover my belongings. It was embarrassing and degrading because I was the only person whose things went out the window. Yes, I felt a certain way about it, but I knew from that point on not to respond or comment in any situation.

On the third day, the verbal abuse began, filled with negative remarks. I received evil looks from my perpetrator, who had a controlling attitude and always wanted to be the center of attention. He was a menace to society and probably still is! One day, while still processing in, we were given many air pressure shots in our arms. I wondered why we were getting so many shots—possibly for mental purposes? I'm not quite sure, but I'm in good health at 52. At that time, I believed we were receiving vaccines for viruses that are now appearing in present times. It felt like the government was experimenting on us.

CHAPTER 4

Who's going to believe a drug addict? Those who use mind-altering substances often find themselves dismissed, but the evil that the government can perpetrate is unimaginable. I can say that because I was once a federal employee.

The breakdown and buildup of basic training was intense. The standard operating procedure (SOP) dictated shaved heads and no facial hair, which felt like another form of degradation. As the days progressed, so did the verbal abuse. I'll refer to my perpetrator as Private S, as I won't use real names for others on this journey.

Private S was particularly negative towards me throughout basic training. We all had our issues, but I suspected he was jealous of me for some reason—maybe it was my appearance. I knew he recognized something extraordinary in me. I was competent and precise, excelling from the very beginning, and that seemed to bother him. Not many soldiers were performing at such a high level.

I vividly remember being jolted awake by the drill sergeants, who were yelling for everyone to get outside. It was snowing, and we were all in our underwear and t-shirts. They kept us out there for at least thirty minutes—part of the training, I guessed. This experience stuck with me, affecting me mentally even back in 1987.

The verbal abuse from Private S continued, and it began to take a toll on my performance. Depression set in, and resentment started to grow. Yet, amid this torment, the drill sergeant also saw something in me. He made me his "house mouse"—a position that required me to maintain his office. Unfortunately, that didn't stop the abuse. Instead, it earned me negative looks from other soldiers, especially Private S.

Feeling the pressure, I started to act out. I began breaking the rules, thinking I had to prove myself to the other soldiers that I was tough. I started sneaking out after hours with other soldiers, making trips to the store for snacks and other contraband. In a way, I was trying to reclaim some sense of control amidst the chaos.

CHAPTER 5

One day, two other soldiers and I decided to break into a candy machine in the activity room. It seemed like harmless fun until someone snitched on us. We were questioned about the incident, and it was concluded that I was one of the participants. As punishment, I received an Article 15 and extra duty.

Looking back, I realize I acted out of peer pressure. I wanted the abuse to stop, but I also craved attention and a sense of belonging. I was exhausted from the torment and felt mentally overwhelmed, not knowing how to escape my situation.

I had always believed we were a team, not enemies. It was mind-boggling to think, could I go to war with someone like Private S, who held an M-16 rifle in his hands? As I write this, I ask myself what Jesus would have done—show compassion and mercy? At that time, those thoughts were far from my mind.

It pains me to reflect on this because I did nothing to provoke Private S's hostility. I've carried this resentment for years, and I can still see his face vividly. If I encountered him today, I would recognize him instantly, even after all these years—amazing, isn't it?

I'm like many others who have endured mental or physical abuse; it doesn't just vanish. The traumatic events replay in the minds of those who continue to suffer. I turned to alcohol and mind-altering substances as an outlet, as did many others, unaware of the long-term damage it would cause. The verbal abuse escalated into physical confrontations; I was pushed in the back and head while in formation, and it felt like Private S was always lurking behind me.

My focus began to fade, and I grew tired of being bullied. Others witnessed the abuse, yet no one spoke up, and neither did I. I was terrified of retaliation, fearing I would be kicked out if I said anything, so I kept my mouth shut. As the situation worsened, I became mentally and physically exhausted. It's important to note that my substance use didn't start until after basic training; this was an escalation I hadn't anticipated.

CHAPTER 6

We completed Basic and AIT in April of 1987, and everyone had orders to their next duty station in two weeks. You could call it a little vacation. During that time, I drank and smoked weed—back then, that's just what we called it. Today, there are a million names for it! I was using both substances socially, but they were just temporary fixes.

As I write this, memories of the assault resurface, and it feels like my perpetrator is right here with me. I can see his face in my mind, just watching me. I don't know if Private S is dead or alive.

Before I delve into the details of the physical assault, I want to express my gratitude to Mr. A. Smith for sharing his story about his trauma and his ongoing recovery from mind-altering substances. I asked A.S. to share his experience, strength, and hope, including any abuse he endured and how his Higher Power has helped him with what he couldn't do for himself.

Sharing your trauma is not easy. Many of us initially say, "I don't want anyone in my business," unaware that opening up can actually release some of the burdens and take power away from the abuse and trauma we've experienced.

The most common outlets for people dealing with trauma are mind-altering substances, often used to forget the incidents that haunt us. Many might wonder why someone is using drugs or drinking excessively without knowing their full story. We get judged in the present, but people forget that we were once law-abiding citizens—at least when we weren't using. Some even bet on how long we'd stay clean.

I struggle with the disease of addiction to mind-altering substances, a result of my trauma. Drugs became a way to block out the things I didn't want to face, complicating my life further as a consequence of my past experiences.

CHAPTER 7

The story of Mr. A.S. is extraordinary. He is a close friend, and here is his testimony. I, A.S., rejoined active duty in January of 1990 while stationed at Fort Lewis in Seattle, Washington. Exactly one year later, I was headed to the Gulf War.

My story begins on a rainy day when my first sergeant called me at my shop. He asked me to reach out to one of my soldiers, Pfc Si, who was on leave. By the end of that day, I noticed that his phone number on the leave form was incorrect. After further review, I found the correct number and began contacting his family. They informed me that he was camping in the mountains and that there was no way to reach him. I left a message with his family, asking them to have him call me as soon as possible and provided all my contact numbers—cell phone, office, and home.

I informed my first sergeant that I hadn't been able to reach Pfc Si and explained that his family said he was in the mountains of California, without any means of communication. At that point, my concern grew, as I wanted to know why Pfc Si had been ordered to report back to base. My first sergeant responded, saying he was to report to Fort Knox to pick up some gear. I was puzzled about what gear was needed.

Then my first sergeant continued, "Pfc Si is going to Southwest Asia." I was shocked. I immediately said, "First sergeant, I volunteer to take his place." I felt prepared for the challenge, and if something were to happen to me in war, my legacy would live on through my three sons. I believed I had been trained by the best.

He told me to take a few days off to think it over. The next day, I returned to his office and said, "I'm ready to go." His reply was, "I told you to take a few days to consult with your wife and kids." After those days passed, I agreed to take on the task.

I received my orders and headed to Fort Knox. I noticed there were many soldiers on the plane. As I started talking to them, I realized we all had something in common—we were all 31-U communications "wire dogs." Wow! The reality of going to war began to sink in. We arrived in Kentucky, where we were met by a bus that would take us to the base. Once there, we began processing and selecting our gear, including rifles and other equipment. We had a mandatory formation to receive our military IDs and dog tags.

CHAPTER 8

It was announced on a certain day that we all had to report to the recreation center, and once inside, we would be escorted in—there was no going back. I recalled not having my shot records because I had been told I wouldn't need them and might lose them during the Gulf War. I was given the option to return to base to be with my family or take every shot up to date.

I had to think about it, and I remember feeling very angry. I sat down to take a load off, and others were saying, "Go home." But then I thought to myself, "I've come this far; I might as well go the rest of the way." So, I took every shot —both arms, buttocks, and even in my mouth. It was unbearable, and we all shared that moment of despair.

We didn't have a plane ready; United Airways was grounded due to an airstrike. "Yeah, buddy!" We all went back to the barracks and partied like it was 1999. All that partying helped distract us from the reality that we might not make it back.

PTSD due to the Gulf War, along with alcohol and drug use, was common among soldiers. We used these substances to cope with the unimaginable sights—dead bodies and the reality of killing another human being. Little did I know I would become addicted to alcohol and drugs.

A few days later, they finally found a plane to fly us over there. We loaded up and off we went. I didn't know if I was happy or sad; mostly, I felt numb. When we arrived at our destination, sirens were blaring: "Gas, Gas, Gas!" The flight attendants rushed us to put on our gas masks. We scrambled off the plane like ants, driven by the chaos on the ground.

When we landed, we were in MOPP level four. We remained in that gear for four hours after departing the plane. I was terrified; I didn't know if I was coming or going, and it affected me mentally. People moving so close to me felt overwhelming. I can still hear the thunder and see the lightning—unbelievable and incredible. I still have nightmares about being run over by a plane or blown up right in front of me. It's amazing that I'm still alive, but the downside is that I suffer from PTSD and addiction to alcohol and mind-altering substances. I surrender to this battle every day.

We stayed in the trenches for hours in MOPP level 4 until we finally received the all-clear command. I thought to myself, "You mean I can take off this soaking wet suit?" Let's not forget about the mask I had on for at least four and a half hours, and I was as hungry as I could be.

That was just the beginning of my torment. I didn't keep records or recordings of what I witnessed—dead Iraqi men, women, and children. At that time, my own children were the same age as those kids, which was hard to swallow.

I witnessed mass burials during my service in the Gulf War, and low-flying aircraft terrified my mind, body, and soul. The loud noise would leave my ears ringing for days. Sandstorms swept across the desert, and I felt incredibly lucky to make it back to the United States. However, the trauma I experienced followed me. I sought treatment in countless facilities across the country for PTSD and substance abuse.

CHAPTER 9

The treatment centers suited me for a short time. By using alcohol and drugs, those were the two things that seemed to help me stop thinking about what I had been through and what I'm going through. My last visit to treatment was at Progressive PHP in Zachary, Louisiana, which sort of made things flare up again. Just being around a huge number of people at one time was scary, but that's PTSD. My life today has changed. I am a part of a fellowship, and it's working for me with the help of others. Today, I see things from a different perspective.

I can very well relate to my friend Mr. A.S. This is how the abuse changed my life. As the verbal abuse continued, one day shortly after, the major physical assault occurred. I was in the back of the barracks on the left side, between the back of a wall locker and a bunk bed. Private S. began to verbally assault me, then he started physically assaulting me. I was trapped. I tried to escape, but the pushing and kicks were excessive.

I didn't recall if other soldiers were looking on. Again, I tried to escape to no avail. Private S. put one hand on the bed and the other on the lockers, lifting himself. He high-kicked me real hard. A window was behind me, and as I was kicked, I turned, thinking it would stop the impact and prevent me from falling out of the window. We were on the second floor. My hands went through the glass window, cutting my right wrist in the process.

I almost fell out the window. I regained myself, and when I turned around, Private S. did not seem to care about what had just happened. I was bleeding, and he saw me bleeding. He asked me if I wanted some more. I was traumatized at that very moment. I did not feel the need to go to the hospital, but my injuries required it. However, I did not want to go for one main reason: I was scared. You might ask, scared of what? I was the victim—yes, get that point, or it will come later. I did not say anything about it throughout basic training and AIT. Maybe things would have been different; maybe I would not have been injured. I thought I was going to get kicked out, and then I would be labeled as a coward. I did not want to be a failure. A lot of negative reasons clogged my mind to remain silent.

What would my family and friends back home say about the whole situation? The CQ (charge of quarters) brought me to the infirmary, and my injuries from the physical abuse required 4 to 5 stitches. It was late when I returned to the barracks with a no physical training profile. I do remember that everyone was sound asleep in their bunks. The following morning, everyone was woken up as usual, and as the day progressed, just about everyone who saw the bandage on my wrist asked me what had happened. I do not remember the excuse I gave them. Whatever I said was a lie, and that gave Private S. the green light to continue the abuse. As I said before, I was traumatized throughout the rest of basic training. Just imagine all the people not saying anything, and those who are being abused at this very moment and not saying anything. We must start saying something—it doesn't matter how you're being abused. Abuse is abuse, period. Abuse will not be tolerated or ignored in today's society.

The other soldiers had to know what was going on and perhaps turned a blind eye to the abuse. Maybe they were like me, afraid to say something. As AIT came to an end, I prayed and hoped that Private S. did not get the same orders I had gotten. "Please, God, do not let that happen!" I said that to myself countless times.

I had orders for Babenhausen, Germany; his were elsewhere. The day we graduated was the last time I saw Private S., and I did not encounter him again in my 4 years of regular Army enlistment. But I did not enlist to be assaulted—verbally or physically—when I raised my right hand to defend this country. I thought we were a team, but we know that one bad person can contaminate everyone in close quarters. Imagine if we were in a war zone, and Private S. and I were in the same foxhole, both holding M-16s, with animosity brewing between us. "It was just a thought at the time." I thank God that it did not materialize.

Everywhere I go, I'm there with my mind and soul. The flashbacks, the constant replay of the incident, the paranoia.

CHAPTER 10

I had orders to report to my duty station two weeks after graduation, and with the incident on my mind, I sought outlets, mostly through alcohol during those two weeks at home. While it provided temporary relief, once the effects wore off, I found myself back at square one.

I was eager to leave Louisiana and board a 747. Arriving at the airport in New Orleans, I felt excitement, particularly about the little bottles of alcohol the flight attendants would serve. I flew from New Orleans to St. Louis, then to New York, and finally to Rhein-Main Air Base in Frankfurt, Germany. Upon arrival, it felt familiar, reminiscent of Bourbon Street.

In the nearby town of Babenhausen, my hard drinking began at popular clubs like Larry's and Upstairs and Downstairs. For about a month, alcohol seemed to work, but my body craved something more. My spirit resisted, but my cravings won out, and I became entrenched in addiction. Although Germany felt familiar, it was also intimidating, as it was new territory for me.

I was welcomed at my unit in Babenhausen, easing my transition. As the days went on, it felt like we partied every weekend, which I thought was normal. My overseas tour felt great as I relied on alcohol to cope with the trauma from basic training. However, as the memories replayed in my mind, alcohol stopped being effective. I began using hashish, convincing myself I needed it to perform my job, despite the ongoing emotional toll from the assault. I pushed those feelings aside, but they never truly left.

The military conducted drug tests, and I managed to avoid detection a few times during my tour. Despite my substance use, I kept my uniform, living quarters, and knowledge of my MOS in good order. I even came in second for Soldier of the Month in the brigade, which led to my selection as the U.S. Colonel's driver. However, I didn’t enjoy this role; it felt isolating, especially when my friends seemed distant upon my return to the unit.

Being the Colonel's driver was tiring. He was tough on me, triggering memories of my past trauma. I struggled with criticism and rejection, which pushed me to request a return to my original unit, and that request was granted. I was relieved to leave, even if it was on a negative note.

I faced financial difficulties, with my ID marked as not eligible for check cashing, which was humiliating. I wrote numerous bad checks, consequences of my own actions. I battled between right and wrong, with my struggles leaning toward the latter. I masked my challenges with alcohol and drugs throughout my overseas tour.

The most positive aspect of that time was the birth of my oldest son. A week before returning to the States, I prayed not to be given a drug test since I had substances in my system. Those 18 months taught me a lot beyond substance use; I learned to take and give orders to accomplish tasks. I returned home as a Specialist E-4, recognized as a top performer in my battalion, but I still felt unfulfilled. I acknowledge that alcohol and drugs played a significant role in my challenges.

CHAPTER II

The flight felt long, and I clearly remember it. They served food, snacks, and, of course, alcohol. Everyone was excited to be heading home, eager to reunite with family. Upon my return, I had a two-week break before reporting back to Ft. Sill—the same duty station where the assault occurred about two years prior. During those two weeks, I celebrated with family and friends, enjoying outdoor barbecues. I had already partied enough overseas to temporarily escape my problems, but the struggles continued.

I noticed upon settling in that there seemed to be two Armies: one in the United States and another overseas. Coming back to the States was a culture shock, compounded by undiagnosed PTSD. I felt depressed, almost as if I had been placed in that unit intentionally—though I couldn't pinpoint by whom, which fueled my paranoia. In my new unit, I had more knowledge due to the intense training I received overseas. I left Babenhausen as an E-4 Specialist and assistant gunner. Shortly after arriving at my new unit, we took a test for a gunner position, and I was one of the few who passed. I was promoted to E-5 and put in charge of five soldiers in my section.

I was a bit confused about the 109 howitzers, as I was more familiar with the 110s, but I learned quickly under my Chief's guidance during fire missions. My biggest fear was encountering my perpetrator; I didn't know where he was stationed, and the memory of the assault lingered in my mind, affecting my job performance. To escape those thoughts, I turned to alcohol and drugs.

When I arrived at my unit at Ft. Sill, the atmosphere was tense. I saw several soldiers walking around with blood-stained clothes; there had been a shooting incident off post, resulting in the death of a fellow soldier who was shot in the head. The soldiers in bloody clothes had been in the car with him. I know the details but can't bring myself to discuss them; it was a tragic situation.

CHAPTER 12

My troubles worsened as I started gambling again, adding to my struggles with alcohol, drugs, and PTSD. At that time, I hadn't yet turned to hard drugs, but gambling was my first issue. My grandfather taught me to play cards when I was about ten, and things escalated once money was involved. He had no way of knowing it would lead to bigger problems, but I don't blame him; I take responsibility for my choices.

I experienced one downfall after another. My no check cashing privileges followed me to the States, but before that was recognized, I opened a checking account at Ft. Sill Federal Credit Union and ordered checks. I remember financing a TV and struggling to repay the loan—an early sign of my unmanageability. My gambling addiction progressed, and it felt like I brought bad luck back from overseas, as I consistently lost. I often called my family, mostly asking for money rather than anything else, which is a common consequence of addiction. Unlike gambling, alcohol and drugs allowed me to forget the assault and other issues I faced.

The unit at Ft. Sill was quite different from what I experienced overseas; it felt more disconnected. I was told to go to the personnel office to have my ID stamped with a no check cashing privilege logo—another embarrassing moment that added to my insecurity. The symptoms of PTSD and the aftermath of the assault continued to weigh on me. I never spoke about the assault because I felt ashamed, insecure, and weak. I wore a mask of denial, hiding my true feelings from anyone I might encounter, which only deepened my depression and anxiety.

I never had a true friend; I didn't know how to be one. I felt I had to give something up for people to like me. While I had acquaintances, I struggled to distinguish between the two. One reason was my constant vigilance after the incident; I was always looking for my perpetrator or anyone who resembled him. This mindset still affects me today, and despite treatment, I have not found effective relief.

CHAPTER 13

The days continued in my unit, and one day my TA-50 (military field gear) went missing from my wall locker, which sent my anxiety soaring. I played a part in this because I had left my locker unlocked. Whether it was theft or a prank, the incident stirred up all sorts of accusations and contempt before any investigation could take place. I was already struggling with financial issues due to drinking, drugs, gambling, writing bad checks, and borrowing money from other soldiers—money I couldn't repay due to my ongoing struggles. I had to report the missing gear to my chain of command.

When my First Sergeant addressed the situation in front of the entire formation, he claimed that I had pawned my TA-50 and that no one had stolen it. I was certain my roommate had taken it, yet no action was taken against him. I had to find a way to replace the gear, but I was already deep in debt, and it felt impossible. It was another embarrassing moment in my life, and I found myself asking, "When will it stop?"

I began to harbor resentment toward everyone and became defiant. As the months passed, I felt trapped in a cycle of problems that seemed never-ending. The combination of bad luck, drinking, drugs, and the PTSD from the assault invaded my thoughts, sleep, and overall well-being. My perception of people and the world drastically changed. I felt lost and lonely, often asking, “Why me, Lord?” with tears and confusion. I started to believe that I was destined to face trials and tribulations throughout my life.

I grew tired—tired of everything. I needed a change, so I enrolled in classes at Cameron University in Lawton, Oklahoma. I took three classes, totaling nine semester hours, which provided a welcome distraction from the unit for half the day. Although this didn’t last long, I was also getting tutored to take another entrance test. I took the test alongside other soldiers and scored a 107, enough to change my MOS from 13-B to 95-B (Military Police). It was a way to prove something to myself, though I knew I would likely end up doing the opposite of what a police officer would do.

After receiving my new MOS, I had orders to go to Ft. Rucker in Alabama for training. I was all set to go, but then I decided to take leave—about 15 days. Returning home to Louisiana was always a challenge for me due to the familiar people, places, and things. While I was on leave, I met another girl and started dating her; she became the mother of my younger son.

I ended up staying on leave longer than I had requested and soon began receiving calls from my chain of command, which I initially ignored. I was in love—or at least I thought I was—and believed she was the answer to all my problems. I felt I didn't need alcohol, drugs, or the urge to gamble. You might wonder about the PTSD, but she made me forget about all that. She became another addiction, though at the time, the relationship felt fulfilling.

As rumors spread that the military was looking for me, I found myself ducking and hiding in different places. I didn't care as long as I was with her, my accomplice. This continued for about a month, during which I drank heavily to cope with the situation. Being AWOL (absent without leave) became my new reality, and fear, isolation, and resentment overwhelmed my mind. To be honest, I had forgotten about my military career and new MOS. My thinking was clouded, so I drove to Ft. Polk, hoping to turn myself in, but that didn't work. I was told I would have to return to Ft. Sill, which I had no desire to do. So, I went back home and continued my reckless behavior for another week.

CHAPTER 14

I finally called my chain of command, and they told me to just come back, which I agreed to do. I caught a Greyhound bus from Thibodaux, LA, to New Orleans, then to Dallas, TX, and eventually reached my destination in Lawton, OK. The bus ride was boring; I just wanted to get there and leave, but they had different plans in mind. I was defiant towards the military, even though it was my own fault for going AWOL. I had thrown my career away, consumed by thoughts of my girlfriend and forgetting the oath I had taken. I felt betrayed by the military after being assaulted by another soldier. The verbal and physical abuse I endured during basic training and AIT left me with resentment towards both my abuser and the military, which drove me to indulge in alcohol, drugs, and gambling —temporary escapes that would lead to addiction.

When I arrived, a sergeant picked me up and said, "Get your gear; you're going to the field!" as if everything was fine. I packed my bags and received more TA-50 gear, as my roommate had stolen my original set. At the field training site, armed with an M-16 and my gear, I resolved to show them how serious I was about leaving the military. Memories of the abuse I had endured weighed heavily on me, especially since it happened just half a mile from this training site.

After everyone settled down for the night, I left my M-16, TA-50, and everything else issued to me behind. I walked about two miles to the military police station and told them I wasn't going to do this anymore. I felt trapped, and my anxiety was at an all-time high. I was exhausted and didn't care about the consequences.

The next morning, I woke up in the MP station, and my unit had already been alerted; the MPs contacted them as soon as I arrived. I didn't care because I was in a fog of confusion. My mental health was unstable, but I hadn't shared my struggles with anyone. The physical assault had left me filled with self-loathing and anger toward everyone around me. A week later, I found myself in front of my chain of command receiving an Article 15.

CHAPTER 15

A week later, I found myself in front of the chain of command receiving my second Article 15. They issued me a Chapter 13, reduced my rank by two grades, assigned me extra duty for a month, and docked my pay. I was already struggling, and this felt like a final blow. It was embarrassing, and I realized I could have avoided all of this if I had just asked for help. My pride got in the way, and my acting out was a desperate cry for assistance. I think people noticed but chose not to intervene, believing it wasn't their business—as long as their lives were in order, everything was fine. My motto became that I didn't need help; once again, pride held me back. I had been taught not to show weakness: "You're a man; you're Army strong. Handle it." Now I was feeling the effects of that conditioning, compounded by PTSD and stress—a perfect recipe for destruction.

I was chaptered out of the military on February 15, 1990, with a general discharge, which was later upgraded, likely thanks to my Higher Power. Finally, I was free from something I thought I wanted to be a part of.

From 1990 to 2017, I worked in various jobs, primarily in security and as a cook in restaurants. My last position was at the VA Hospital in New Orleans, Louisiana, where I worked as a level 4 cook from February 5, 2017, until I resigned for medical reasons on August 26, 2018.

When I discharged from the military in 1990, my girlfriend was still by my side. I enrolled in a course at Delta College in Houma, Louisiana, focusing on security and private investigation. After completing the course, we moved to Atlanta, Georgia, staying with her cousin until we could find our own place. While drinking was part of our lifestyle, she wasn't an alcoholic—I was. At that time, hard drugs like cocaine hadn't entered my life yet, but I felt a sense of normalcy on the outside. Inside, I still felt like a failure. I had yet to share the details of the assault with anyone, including her, which had profoundly changed my life and perspective on the world. Despite this, I found some happiness being with her; my focus on her helped distract me from the pain and memories.

While living in Clarkston, GA, with her cousin, we both found jobs quickly, which was a relief. During the week, we didn't drink much unless we went out to clubs or bars. However, as time went on, I started venturing out more, often visiting bars and strip clubs like "Magic City." My drinking escalated, but I didn't see it as a problem—yet again, that word loomed.

I wasn't gambling or using drugs at that point, and later I would learn that alcohol is, in fact, a drug, a lesson reinforced in various programs and treatment centers.

I should mention the car I bought while in the service—a 1990 Dodge Shadow from E.C. Chrysler in Lawton, OK. This came after the repossession of my Nissan Hardbody truck from G.L. Nissan in Thibodaux. I had a co-signer for that loan, and I owe them an apology for not fulfilling my end of the deal. That was one of my lowest points after leaving the military.

After I resolved my AWOL situation, I left the Dodge Shadow at home and took a bus back to Ft. Sill. When I ETS'd from the military, that car was waiting for me. It was how my girlfriend and I got to Atlanta.

CHAPTER 16

I had stopped paying the car note two months earlier. When I bought that car, I didn't read the contract thoroughly—or rather, I didn't care to read it at all. In fine print, it stated, "The car shall not be removed from the state until fully paid for." They contacted me numerous times about the vehicle, and I even called them, asking them to come get it, letting them know it was broken down.

Eventually, I bought a Mazda RX-7 from a buy-here-pay-here dealership, and they finally came to pick up the Dodge Shadow. I thought I was free from that burden. However, while driving to her cousin's house, we were stopped by the police for a non-working tail light. They ran a check on my driver's license, and a warrant came back from Lawton, OK. I couldn't believe it. When I was taken to DeKalb County Jail, I learned that the warrant was for "removing property without consent from the owner." I protested that they had already taken the car, but the warrant still stood. This was a consequence of my past failures to handle my responsibilities properly.

I was extradited to Lawton, OK, from Decatur, GA. The worst part was the 12-hour car ride. Honestly, I cried most of the way; I was scared and overwhelmed. I learned a valuable lesson from that incident: always read contracts thoroughly and have someone else review them before signing. At that time, I might have been under the influence, believing I knew everything, which led to another poor decision and its resulting consequences.

The jail cell in Lawton was small and uncomfortable, but wasn't that the point? The next day, I went to court, got a bond, and my mom bailed me out from Louisiana. I took the bus back to Atlanta and then drove to Lawton for three months to attend court until the situation was resolved.

After returning to Atlanta, my girlfriend and I moved back to Louisiana, then back to Atlanta, and again to Louisiana. Throughout this time, I continued to drink heavily, while she was pregnant with my youngest son. I was happy about having my child—my third with three different women—but I still struggled with my addiction.

Addiction doesn't care about anyone or anything. We lived together for a while, then separated and reconciled multiple times. About a year before our final separation, I started selling drugs. Crack cocaine was in high demand, and it seemed everyone was selling it. Before I started, I had asked my brother why he was involved in that lifestyle. God bless his soul; I don't remember his answer, but soon after, I found myself doing the same thing. I didn't recognize the implications of selling drugs and eventually faced the consequences.

I made money, but I also felt guilt. I hadn't started using drugs yet, but I wondered why there was such high demand for them. This was around 1995. My gambling and drinking escalated, which is typical for addiction. During that time, most drug dealers engaged in heavy drinking and gambling. I remember thinking, "Everything seems to be going great."

That was my addiction speaking—deluding me into believing everything was fine. Yes, we had a baby boy, a house, food, cars, money, and designer clothes, but none of that equated to true happiness. I was emotionally dependent on her, but during our separations, I was unfaithful, engaging with other women regardless of their substance use.

CHAPTER 17

I enjoyed the feeling of sex and anything else that made me feel good. I recognized I had an addictive personality. When I discovered she was interested in someone else, I couldn't handle it. In my mind, I was obsessed; she felt like a drug I couldn't let go of. After our last separation, I sought out distractions to forget her and cope with the loss.

My life changed dramatically when I first tried crack cocaine in the summer of 1995. I remember exactly where I was and who was there. The moment I inhaled from a makeshift pipe, everything shifted: my problems seemed to vanish, I felt invincible, and I believed I had all the answers. I thought I had become a god, so delusional was I at that moment. I convinced myself I didn't need anyone—only the drug, which I believed was enhancing my thoughts.

Little did I know what awaited me; only God knew my fate. After that initial experience, I told myself it would only be a weekend indulgence, but crack had other plans. I didn't realize I had a choice at that time. We grew closer, spending more time together, and the drug's allure deepened. It reminded me of my ex-girlfriend, a roaming spirit who never stayed. I fell in love with the drug, but it was never in love with me.

I longed for a faithful relationship, yet I was met with years of misery. From that day forward, I encountered a whirlwind of problems—obsession, compulsive behaviors, mental health struggles, family issues, manipulations, legal troubles, and financial chaos—all exacerbated by the insanity of continued drug and alcohol use, along with gambling.

My PTSD stemmed from the physical assault, and I masked my feelings with substances. But the trauma never left; it lingered, waiting for my mind to clear.

CHAPTER 18

I didn't want to think about my perpetrator or the assault, and if that meant medicating myself to avoid feeling anything, it seemed like a good idea—until it inevitably backfired.

Defects & Problems

My thinking was faulty; I struggled to understand myself, others, and the world around me. I was fixated on avoiding the past, particularly the abuse that had caused my PTSD. Alcohol and drugs became my means of relief, leading to addiction. The urges were excruciating when I didn't have them, and anxiety would consume me until I gave in. Despite my good intentions, I found myself thinking the opposite—I felt like everyone was against me.

The assault, depression, anxiety, addictions, and PTSD plagued my mind. Drugs became a temporary coping mechanism, but I always needed more to escape my relentless thoughts. That was the only outlet I knew at the time.

My Obsession

The persistent idea that I had to have my drug by any means necessary consumed me. The drug was embedded in my consciousness, and the obsession replayed itself endlessly. I felt like I was losing my mind, unable to stop. I formed bonds with substances, glorifying them to the point where nothing else mattered. If I didn't get my drug, I would shed tears—it had that much influence over my life.

My Compulsiveness

I felt compelled to use drugs every single moment. After each use, the urge to do it again became overwhelming. Alcohol primed me for my drug of choice, and I took everything to the extreme. I pushed myself until I was exhausted, completely depleted.

I would go anywhere for drugs, refusing to stop until I found what I was seeking or a victim to further my mission. For me, everything went from 0 to 100 in an instant. While others operated at a normal pace, I was on overdrive. One of my past sponsors reminded me that learning to slow down is a lifelong process.

My Mental Health

My mental health issues took me to a different dimension, where I felt everyone was out to harm me, especially my family. I became skeptical of them and was cautious about accepting anything they offered. The greatest fear I faced was using drugs and not being able to return from that dark place; the thought of encountering demonic and evil spirits in that dimension was terrifying. Drugs opened a door to a world that some never return from, either physically or mentally.

My Family

I stole from my family—mentally and physically—to support my addiction. This led to mistrust, but when I was using, I didn't want to be around them. I felt out of place among those who weren't using. I knew they cared, but I didn't want them to witness my struggles. As my addiction progressed, their feelings became irrelevant to me; all that mattered was my need to escape. I used more to mask my emotions, fully aware I was hurting them, but I couldn't stop.

They thought I wanted to live this way, believing that a pill or treatment would solve my problems. They didn't understand addiction fully; they had ideas but lacked the insight into the true nature of the diseases.

Little did they know, it doesn't work quite like that. The key was that I wasn't willing to stop at that point. Instead of asking me how it all started or educating themselves for a better understanding, one person said it had to "run its course." My understanding came slowly—only when I immersed myself in a fellowship did I begin to learn, even just a little, about my disease of addiction. I had to ask myself what led me to use mind-altering substances to escape my feelings and perceptions about the past. Recovery is a lifelong process, and by being honest, open-minded, and willing to do what's necessary, I'm well on my way.

My Relationships

All my relationships were one-sided, focused solely on what I could gain. I was selfish and self-centered, even as I claimed to love everyone, especially my children. I started using drugs at age 26, and they say that's when your emotional growth stops. Now, at 52, I feel like I'm just beginning to catch up. Yes, I look mature on the outside, but inside, I'm still that little boy who feels lost and lonely. Being an adult and acting like one are two different things. I wasn't truly being an adult; I was playing a role, and that led to many detrimental mistakes.

My relationships with family and so-called friends fluctuated. When I was sober for short periods, things were okay, but once the using started, everything fell apart. I tried to reconcile, but people don't forget the damage I caused. I thought apologies would be enough, but I often repeated the same mistakes, expecting them to accept my regrets. I had to learn the hard way that regaining trust takes time and effort.

When I was doing well in recovery, I realized it wasn't enough to simply say I would change; I had to follow through with action.

My Communication

To others, my interactions were often harsh. While I was kind to those who fulfilled my needs—especially drug dealers, who had what I wanted—I communicated my feelings primarily through writing. I documented everything I was going through and those I believed contributed to my downfall. I felt law enforcement was part of my misfortune, but the truth is, I was my own worst enemy. I was often a target, even when standing next to a known drug dealer. Those who spread misinformation about me and participated in my failures are no longer around; God makes things possible.

God was communicating with me 100% of the time, and I truly believe that. I've come to understand that while we may be made in His image, we lack many of His attributes. During my years of communicating with God, I would often ask, "Why me, God?" I would cry, curled up in a ball, hoping He would end my suffering. Yet, through it all, I endured with His help. I may have been weak at times, but I continued to survive the best way I knew how. I've been through a lot, and I'm not afraid to share my story and what God is doing in my life. Today, I don't ask God "why"; I know the answer.

My Lies

I lied about many things, to many people—on job applications, about my personal life, and even to my family and children. It felt good to say something positive at the time, but I wasn't true to myself, so how could I be true to others? I believed my own lies, despite knowing they wouldn't lead to anything righteous.

The negativity I expressed about others wasn't aligned with God's will for my life. I built my foundation on lies, creating a house of deceit that eventually overflowed into my life and the lives of those around me.

I now understand that telling the truth makes life easier for me and for those who come into my presence. I've learned not to jump to conclusions; instead, I investigate the facts, and the facts are truths.

My Finances

My finances were unmanageable. I didn't know much about money, but I certainly knew how to spend it when I had it. In the beginning of this book, I mentioned the suspension of my check-cashing privileges in the military —this was a warning sign of bigger issues. I had at least four cars repossessed and gave a few away during my addiction. I faced warrants for bounced checks, both legitimate and illegitimate loans, and creditors hunted me down. I intended to do the right thing, but I didn't know how to repay what I owed.

When I started using drugs heavily, most of my earnings went toward my addiction. My credit score has been in the low 500s for over 30 years. The absurdity was that I often spent money on drugs before I even received my paycheck. My financial troubles continued to haunt me. Recently, I've realized the importance of taking care of my responsibilities—no one else will do it for me. Through my experiences, I've learned valuable lessons. Psalms 37:21 says, "The wicked borrows and does not pay back, but the righteous is gracious and gives." If we don't want to be seen as wicked by God, we must repay our debts; restitution brings freedom.

My Behavior

My behavior was radical, especially under the influence of mind-altering substances. Even as a child, I never felt normal. I always wanted what I wanted—immediately. I often went along with my peers, not stepping into a leadership role. I made mistakes simply because I didn't know any better. My behavior wasn't typical; I acted in ways that were childish.

The tantrums and drama I displayed were witnessed by others, yet I justified my actions. Before I started using substances, I already had issues with my behavior, and drugs only intensified them. I was at war with myself and others, feeling like everyone owed me something—an apology, recognition, or praise. This expectation caused me numerous problems in the workplace and in social settings. I realized that by avoiding mind-altering substances, I had a chance to work on my behavior and avoid falling into a hopeless state of mind.

My Insanity

I was truly insane. How could I keep doing the same things over and over, knowing they would produce negative results? I became accustomed to the pain my addiction brought. When my money and resources were gone, I'd come up with brilliant ideas to get what I wanted. Addicts are incredibly resourceful when it comes to obtaining and using drugs. I rarely knew what day it was or where I was. At times, I didn't even know if I was in Louisiana, Mississippi, Alabama, Georgia, or Florida—it was all a blur.

Sometimes I had to stop and think about where I was. I found myself in places I didn't remember and others I did, mostly landmarks in different states. Looking back, it was scary, yet it never stopped me from returning to what I had done best for 26 years: using substances, with only a few months of sobriety scattered in between. I thought true longevity was impossible.

I was operating in a state of insanity, which led to a lot of trouble with the law and others. The mental stress I put on my body and spirit was immense. I learned that I could predict the outcomes of my actions, whether negative or positive. With the grace of God, I have faith that I can make the right choices, staying calm and insightful—that's what I continually pray for.

My Denial

As I mentioned before, my denial was profound. I believed I wasn't an alcoholic or an addict, convincing myself I could control my behavior. "I've got this," I would say. I thought there was nothing wrong with me; everyone else was the problem. I was just trying to have fun and not hurting anyone!

While that sounded good, the truth was I was hurting myself and those who cared for me, especially my loved ones. My denial almost killed me. If I had continued down that path, I wouldn't have gotten the help I needed. It took many treatment sessions to shatter that denial. I often questioned, "Why am I here?" I wasn't there to play or to pretend I was fine; I was there because I had a serious problem—notice I didn't say "had." It was a problem I didn't know how to manage until I accepted help. That's when I became open to change.

I didn't just struggle with mind-altering substances; I also didn't know how to live life on life's terms. I did whatever I wanted, dismissing anyone who tried to guide me. I thought I knew what was best for my life, but that realization brought me to a critical question: Why was I sitting in a treatment center? The answer was clear: I needed help, and that's where my denial finally ended.

CHAPTER 19

I had been using substances for a long time and never faced any major health issues—at least, I thought I hadn't. My body was mostly numb from the alcohol and drugs, so I didn't really feel anything, physically or emotionally. However, I distinctly remember the emotional turmoil when I didn't have access to substances and couldn't find a way to get them. That's when I felt truly exhausted.

During my brief periods of sobriety in treatment centers and hospitals, I often became very ill, even though I had felt fine just hours earlier—typically because I was high. I suspect the abrupt stop in using shocked my body. After a week-long binge, my system was unprepared for basic necessities like food and water. In the hospital, when I tried to eat, my body couldn't handle it. The addiction had trained me to survive on drugs for days, sometimes weeks, with only a little water here and there. In my mind, those essentials were far less important than getting high.

As a result of my long-term substance use, I now face several health issues: I'm pre-diabetic, have high cholesterol, and suffer from tardive dyskinesia due to the medication I take for my mental health. My body aches regularly, and I deal with stomach problems like GERD, along with a host of other issues. These conditions primarily stem from my alcohol and drug use, but they also relate back to the physical assault that caused my PTSD, which led me to rely on substances as a coping mechanism. The reality is that using drugs and alcohol has long-term effects on both mental and physical health, even for those who haven't abused them to the extent I did.

As I mentioned, my long history of alcohol and drug use is not something to brag about. You might think, "You haven't learned anything after all this." On February 16, 2021, I checked into Thibodaux General Hospital in Thibodaux, Louisiana. It was Fat Tuesday (Mardi Gras Day), but all festivities were canceled due to the COVID-19 pandemic. I entered the detox phase on the fourth floor—though I'm not sure which one—and it was yet another attempt to get well. They promised to help me, but I still held on to my own ideas about how I wanted to be treated and where I wanted to go after detox. Again, I was trying to make decisions when I wasn't really capable of doing so.

I was reluctant to return to the New Orleans VA, but that's where they wanted to send me. Fear set in; I dreaded that place. We had a troubled history together, and the doctors at Thibodaux General insisted I go. So, I swallowed my pride and agreed. I was transported to the New Orleans VA that night. Surprisingly, I was welcomed, but in my mind, I was still holding on to past grievances, illustrating just how mentally ill I had become, on top of my substance use. I was the only one stuck in the past, especially regarding my previous visits. I harbored resentment, feeding into it between visits, convinced that they wouldn't help me. It felt like I had been blackballed due to my ongoing litigation against the VA, but most of it was about my own insecurities. I was wallowing in self-pity, thinking I deserved special treatment and respect—even though I was sicker than I had ever been.

I stayed at the VA Medical Center in New Orleans from February 17 to February 26, 2021. I was discharged with the intention of immediately entering the next phase of my treatment, vowing to myself that I was done with alcohol and drugs.

My vehicle was waiting for me in the VA parking lot. As I left New Orleans to head to the next phase of my treatment in Zachary, Louisiana, I made a big mistake: I called my drug dealer, asking him for money for gas. The truth was, I had enough gas. We met at a car wash, and after he gave me $30, I couldn't help but ask him for drugs. The addiction spoke through me: "Just let me get one." I had said that countless times before, knowing that one would inevitably lead to many more. Soon, I would be broke, then deep in debt, caught in a cycle of insanity. But this time, my dealer said, "No, go to treatment."

I was furious that he said no and he drove off. With the $30 he gave me, I bought drugs from someone else, leading to about 12 hours of pure hell. I ran out of money and began to rack up debt for drugs, riding around the city using until my gas tank ran low. Eventually, I ran out of gas in my own neighborhood, which was incredibly embarrassing. Nobody stopped to help me, but that same dealer later gave me $5 for gas. I managed to catch a ride to the gas station, but even after filling up, my vehicle still wouldn't start. I faced another issue with the battery, and again, no one stopped to assist me—not even a family member. I felt a heavy burden of resentment, and I learned that resentment breeds all kinds of spiritual illness.

At that moment, I hated my neighborhood and was furious with myself and everyone else. I worked on my truck throughout the night, determined to get it started. By morning, February 27, 2021, I had walked a total of about two miles back and forth to recharge my battery. After 12 hours of insanity, I was ready to quit alcohol and drugs for good. That experience was a brutal reminder of the vicious cycle of my addiction.

Around 6 AM, I finally got my vehicle started. Right then and there, I knew God was with me; there was no way I could have made it out of that situation without Him. The same was true for all my past struggles in and out of addiction. Jails and institutions are miserable cycles, but God was present, even when I didn't recognize it.

"Thank you, God," were the first words that came out of my mouth when the vehicle started. From that moment on, I knew my Creator is real. I heard a strong voice urging me: "Go, go, go!" So, I hurriedly drove to my home, grabbed some clothes, and asked three family members for gas money. Each one said they didn't have any. I thought to myself, "Really? You don't have even a dollar?" But that same voice encouraged me to "still go, go, go." I set out on my journey in faith, listening to that voice, with only a quarter tank of gas. I knew that would get me 15 miles or so, but my destination was 75 miles away. I had faith that God had already placed someone along my path to help me reach my destination.

CHAPTER 20

I was 14 miles in, having reached Vacherie, Louisiana, when I pulled into a gas station and asked the first person I saw, "Sir, do you have $5 for gas?" You might wonder why I only asked for $5, knowing it wouldn't get me to my destination. But it didn't matter what I asked for—God had already set a plan in motion. I don't remember the person's name, but he told me to pull up to the pump. I felt elated and grateful as he pumped gas into my truck. "It's rough out here," I admitted, and he replied, "Yes, it can get pretty tough." I thanked him for the gas, and he simply said, "You're welcome." This experience reinforced my belief that God is good—not just sometimes, but all the time, especially in moments of need. When I looked at the gas gauge, it showed half full—more than enough to reach my destination.

My phone was off because I hadn't paid the bill; that was on me, as I prioritized drugs over everything else. I made it to treatment the old-fashioned way, demonstrating just how badly I wanted recovery. I followed signs and asked gas station attendants and other people at red lights for directions. I arrived at the treatment center around 10 AM on February 27, 2021, but I actually passed the center and had to pull over to clean myself up on the side of the road. I was still under the influence; the last 12 hours of using had taken their toll. I knew it was time to surrender and end the madness.

When I checked in with the staff, I finally felt safe, as if a heavy burden had been lifted off my shoulders. I rested for the day, but soon reality set in, and I began to confront the wreckage I had caused. I had kept quiet about the abuse I suffered years ago, thinking I could manage it alone. If I had sought help sooner, perhaps I wouldn't have found myself in this situation. Masking my pain with alcohol and drugs was tragic; it was the only way I knew to escape my struggles. Now, it's my responsibility to confront and correct those issues with God's help. I vowed to let nothing interfere with my recovery from the physical assault that caused my PTSD. Recovery is my focus now, supported by my Higher Power and those whom God has placed in my life on this journey.

CHAPTER 21

Here are 14 positive attributes I call my anchors, helping me stay grounded one day at a time. They might be useful for anyone trying to make a change in their life. With God or your chosen Higher Power, anything is possible, and when something is possible, it means I have a chance for it to materialize. This is not the end; it's the beginning of a new life.

I asked myself, "Why am I here?" This was the first question I faced when starting treatment. Initially, I had many reasons for being there. Reflecting on the past, I thought I was there to learn how to use substances successfully, to regain my health and appearance, to save money, or to find a partner. I was focused on everything but my own problems, often justifying my presence for my family, my children, or my job—anyone but myself.

When I entered treatment on February 27, 2021, I honestly revisited the question of why I was there. I wanted to get well, but I needed to go beyond my previous attempts. I had to confront my past actions and the reasons behind my recovery efforts. It felt like I had come full circle.

I remember when I was manipulative, and I could tell when I was being honest. Others could see it too, because we are somewhat alike. My motto became about bettering myself. I was there to learn, to share my experiences and acknowledge how I had been a menace to society. Those realizations fueled my desire to change my life without relying on alcohol and drugs to cope. Wherever you are in life, ask yourself honestly, "Why am I here?" Reflect on your past; it can motivate you to do better.

My Spirituality

Today, my spirituality consists of reading the Bible, meditation, prayer, staying humble, and practicing the 12 spiritual principles of my recovery program. I strive to maintain conscious contact with my Higher Power, whom I choose to call God. We may have different views on a Higher Power, but I believe it's a personal choice. I respect what others believe; I've retired from debating the topic. I know what works for me, and I trust you know what works for you. Ultimately, I believe we all seek the same destination: a place of freedom, love, peace, and happiness. Spirituality is vital for me; my flesh often craves what it wants. I focus on the word "override"—elevating my spirit over my flesh has helped my spiritual growth. I recognize that these two are often in conflict. I pray throughout the day. I'm far from perfect, and sometimes I forget who's in charge, but my spirit reminds me of my Higher Power's attributes.

My Higher Power gives me strength to refocus, and meditation brings me peace, especially in quiet surroundings. When I meditate outdoors, I connect with nature—I feel the wind, hear the leaves rustling, and become aware of my body and breath. In essence, I establish conscious contact with my spirit and my Higher Power. Reading and writing also help me immensely. When I ask for strength, my Higher Power works through me, expressing love. It's not about me; it's about sharing how spirituality can save lives.

My Focus

For me, focus is essential; it's my center of interest at this point in my life. The most important thing to me is my recovery. This is not a short-term focus; it's about longevity and finding contentment, which is crucial for my life—and possibly yours, too. At one time, my focus was on everything but improving myself. I concentrated on material things and how others perceived me, but I've come to understand that only God can and will judge me, ideally by my actions and the work I do in faith. When I fall short, I don't worry; I always learn something new from each experience, and I humbly accept it. I will never give up! Without recovery and applying spiritual principles to my life, I would have no life. So, I choose recovery and to live by these principles.

When I focus on God, He translates His will and attributes into my life. I am inspired to create positivity, which encourages others to see their salvation. We were once lost, but now we focus on what will make us free.

Recovery Groups, Classes, and Meetings

These are the core of my recovery. Initially, it was hard to digest the information. I didn't understand much about recovery, but consistent attendance helped me, and it may help you too. I would never convey information I don't fully understand about recovery, as it could cost someone their life—misinformation is dangerous. I trust the insights I gained from professionals in the field, recognizing that instructors, therapists, and doctors have degrees and expertise in mental health and substance abuse. It was essential for me to show up, participate, and share my opinions. Now, learning seems easier; it was challenging when I was younger, likely due to my 26 years of substance use and treatment. Retaining information was hard at first, but once the haze cleared, I began to see things more clearly. Throughout my time in treatment, I was a good student with strong attendance and participation, but once I left, everything I learned often faded. A counselor once asked what I did first when I got out of treatment, and I replied, "I went back home, to my neighborhood"—my old playgrounds. He said, "That's part of the problem." That was a major eye-opener, revealing that I hadn't applied what little I had learned.

Today, with my Higher Power and spiritual principles, I strive to remain honest, open-minded, willing, and teachable, with a desire to help others. With that mindset, I'm well on my way to a bright future and a better understanding of how to live life on life's terms.

My Honesty

Honesty is a significant part of my recovery, though it has been a character defect since birth. Learning to be honest was challenging, but the truth brings freedom and liberation. When I'm not honest, it affects my mind and body, creating issues I must recover from daily. It's easy to fall into dishonesty. My recovery hinges on my ability to be honest. If I can't be honest, I can't recover from anything, especially concerning mind-altering substances. Lying was an ingrained pattern I needed to break. I was 100% dishonest about certain things during my first treatment, but today, after two decades, I can say I'm more honest than I've ever been, with room for further growth.

When untruthful conversations arise, I have the right to challenge them. Being honest with myself allows me to be honest with you. Today, I never jump to conclusions without investigation; that's a skill that must be learned from the heart. Dishonesty is a character defect I had to confront. The good news is that we all have the capacity for honesty if we work toward it.

My Open-Mindedness

Looking back, I realize how closed-minded I was; I struggled to accept other perspectives. My views always seemed right, regardless of proof. That attitude stunted my growth for a long time. I resisted correction because I was selfish and self-centered. Those character defects prevented me from seeing things from others' viewpoints. Now, I'm excited about being open-minded; I can consider different perspectives and incorporate them into my own views. It's like grafting different trees into one—now I'm diverse. We can have conversations without debate, fostering harmony and peace.

My Willingness

I'm motivated to say, "I'm going to do this." I'm determined now in ways I wasn't in the past. I am stable and resolute. I used to be willing only sometimes, but that willingness was fleeting. Today, I'm willing to do whatever is necessary to remain free in body, mind, and soul. The most important aspect is my willingness to incorporate spiritual principles into my life. I can speak about this, but without action, it means nothing. I remember being depressed often, doing only the minimum, but that was always a start. Things do change and get better. To be successful in anything, willingness to do what's necessary is essential. The first step must be taken, and I must continue to be willing. It's my choice—an individual choice. Willingness is my internal motivation, given by God, to accomplish what lies ahead.

Remaining Teachable

Going back to school? It never ends. I strive daily to listen and absorb what is being said. It wasn't that I had selective hearing; it was about what I could comprehend and relate to based on my experiences. I'm not shutting the door on my past; I use it as a reflection for navigating current situations—deciding what to do and what not to do. I consider the consequences and outcomes. I must remain open-minded, though I'm not perfect. I always ask my Higher Power for help. When God created me and you, in His eyes, we are perfect. I used to believe I was perfect, pretending for most of my life, but I had shut out the sunlight of God, depriving my soul of nourishment. I had to heed the advice of those who came before me: "Take the cotton out of your ears and put it in your mouth." I have a problem with that because I love to talk! I once told my mother that my mouth hurt from biting my tongue; she quickly replied, "Brian Keith, you talk too much." That was my cue to listen more.

The Fellowship

Fellowshipping is vital; I was alone in my addiction. Today, I have a close circle of friends with similar experiences and interests. I remember how I used to fellowship during previous recovery attempts—to get something out of others or satisfy my own needs. I was doing it for all the wrong reasons, which caused more problems. Today, I fellowship for meaningful reasons: it's a part of my recovery program, and I can't do this alone. I need others who understand me. This doesn't exclude those without addiction in my life; we all need each other, regardless of race, creed, or sexual orientation—God created us all. I've learned acceptance: I accept who you are and what you believe, even if I don't agree with everything. I respect your views and hope for the same respect in return. When I fellowship, I learn from others, and we share our experiences, strength, and hope.

Service Work

I understand the importance of service, even if it's just opening the door at a meeting, making coffee, or cleaning up afterward. But it goes beyond meeting rooms. I believe helping others is part of our calling. To be honest, I'm still learning about service work. During my last treatment attempt, I made coffee for meetings and helped set up the room. Within a month, I was trusted enough to be voted in as a General Service Representative

Spiritual, Mental, and Physical Health

If I'm not spiritually fit, nothing will go right because I would be acting out of self-will. I say this from experience; I'm not religious, but I pray and believe in a Higher Power. Throughout the day, I strive to maintain conscious contact with God, although I'm not perfect. God often corrects me and allows me to learn from my mistakes. I've learned that when I operate in Brian's will instead of God's, I get Brian's results rather than God's. When I listen to my spirit, it guides me in making the right choices.

In the beginning, my mental health was a mess, but after two months in treatment, things cleared up. Mind-altering substances significantly impact mental health, and EMDR therapy has helped with my PTSD. However, the memories remain. My past experiences have taught me about myself and my reactions to people, places, and things. It's essential to be mentally competent, with or without prescribed medication, as this is a personal goal to strive for.

My physical health was poor, but now I'm learning to eat right and stay active, which prevents many illnesses. Physical activity helps reduce my stress and anxiety, and I feel 100% better since I adopted a healthier lifestyle.

Fun and Leisure Time

What would recovery be without happiness and fun? Today, I try activities I once thought I didn't like, realizing I need to explore morally positive experiences, not those that could harm me. Since entering recovery, I've visited places I always dreamed about—opportunities that would have been impossible while in the grips of addiction. I often reflect on where happiness and leisure fit into my past; in my addiction, I was often unaware of their existence. I lived for myself, with time feeling fleeting. Now, I'm open with God about everything I've done. I have no secrets, and I find joy in living life on my own terms, engaging in activities that bring me happiness.

Business Minded

In recovery, we discover our brilliance and the potential to change the world. Our ideals must move forward from our hearts and minds. God instills our passions, so when doubts arise, we must ignore them. God has equipped us to fulfill His purpose. I remain dedicated to this calling, knowing I have the mind of Christ and the ability to create and succeed.

Live and Let Live

In the past, I struggled with living fully, often wishing for death to escape the pain of addiction. That mindset was overwhelming, and I recognize that taking my own life would have been selfish. Everyone deserves a chance at a long and prosperous life. I want to uplift those I encounter, even when I face my own struggles. I remind myself to choose joy despite challenges, grateful for the gifts of life and a discerning spirit.

Recovery After Treatment

This is when I apply the skills learned from classes, groups, meetings, fellowship, service work, and step work. Living by spiritual principles, I help others and accept help myself. Today, I remain honest, open-minded, and willing to pursue a beneficial path. If you're reading this while in treatment or returning from a relapse, know you have a choice. Keeping things simple and taking suggestions can make recovery realistic. A mentor once told me, "When you stop doing the necessary things for your recovery, you no longer want it." That insight was invaluable. I truly hope the contents of this book support you on your recovery journey. May God bless you beyond your imagination!

WRITTEN BY

Brian Keith Redmond

&

1

Short Story

by

Alfred Smith

" BIGGER"

THE WORLD IS BIG!

AFTERWORD

Some think Covid-19 is bigger, pandemics come and go, maybe man made but It's not my place to say so. There Is a time for everything yes under the sun, remember in a bubble the Lakers won. When scientist put rubber to the road, we got figures, I know the work was rigorous, with still a little fear, it's been way over the 2020 year, let's keep some of the mandates, this virus is real. With transparency, it's apparent to me, I'm gonna get vaccinated, whatever it might do to me, that's my opinion but we all want to be free, gathering and chattering, less symptoms of PTSD, yes It tried to get the best me. without help, I'm surely to be in defeat, so I strive above the negativity. I vow to put in the work, because my addiction lurks and that physical assault still hurts, so I now live by principles, that are so indispensable. I'm so complicated in a good way, at this point in my life it's no fight, "I surrender", because I remember the pain, surely in the years to come, I want be the same man and that's only If I stick to my HIGHER POWER PLANS!

www.ingramcontent.com/pod-product-compliance
Lightning Source LLC
LaVergne TN
LVHW010118170826
845678LV00012B/2474

* 9 7 9 8 8 9 5 6 9 8 0 8 2 *